SUNG TO SHAHRYAR

Poems from The Book of the Thousand Nights and One Night.

by

E. POWYS MATHERS.

Author of Coloured Stars, The Garden of Bright Waters, etc.

DARF PUBLISHERS LIMITED
LONDON
1986

FIRST PUBLISHED 1925
NEW IMPRESSION 1986

ISBN 1 85077 146 4

Printed and bound in Great Britain
by A. Wheaton & Co. Ltd, Exeter, Devon

NOTE

*These verses have been selected from The
Book of The Thousand Nights and One
Night which was rendered from the literal
version of Dr. J. C. Mardrus*

"Love is birds among fruit and running water."

CONTENTS

PLACES

BIRDS

DEATH

BATHS

H A M M A M of delicious bathing,
Admirable, sense-defying ;
Silver vapour, scented plaything,
Half to die and after dying
Half to live in sleepy swathing,
Hammam of delicious bathing.

L O V E has filled my soul with wine and gold
But I keep them for him
Who has pastured the black scorpions of his hair
Upon my heart.

He is a sword,
A bow with black arrows,
He is a white song written in tears of roses.

Come with me to the bath, beloved,
Nard shall burn his faint blue kisses about us
And I will lie singing upon your heart.

B

3.

AS THE hammam fire renews
Ageing heart and tired thews,
I lie and love the kissing air,
The brightness of the basins there,
Falling water, falling light
On the marble hard and white,
Rooms of shadows filled with blue
Wreaths of incense, driven through
By a breeze which carries too
All the sweet the furnace sends
From the bodies of my friends.
Eternal shade, eternal heat,
There's analogy complete,
Hammam, dark for all your fires,
Of my soul and my desires.

4.

THEY welcomed me with silent smiling,
    They warmed me at their fire,
I found their manners most beguiling
    At the hammam.

FOOD

I.

On a Silver Table.

CAST down your eyes, lift up your souls,
Dig spoons into the great sauce bowls.
Eat roast and fried and boiled and grilled,
Eat jams and jellies, warmed and chilled.
Eat quails cooked golden to the minute,
Eat nut-fed lamb with raisins in it.
Who would the warm stout capon blame,
Date-coloured with judicious flame,
Because he could not sing or fly ?
(He eats the better.)   Nor can I. . .
The golds of man are manifold
But Allah made this kabab's gold ;
He made this purslane salad sup
The soul of olives from a cup ;
He set these twin and ponderous fish
To lie on mint leaves in a dish. . .
I will be silent now and eat
A meal which poets shall repeat
In songs of cooking, sound and sage,
Down all the hungry roads of age.

STS-B

2.

On a Tray.

HOT
Meats,
Cheese,
Fish,
And
Sweets ;
Bake,
Roaſt,
And
Stew ;
Please
Take
What
Moſt
You
Wish.

3.

Fried Fish.

AH, AH, the delicate flesh,
  Little birds flying under the sea,
Until they are caught in a mesh, a mesh,
  And bought and brought to me !

The oil is a lover who gilds them with gold,
  Amorous is the dish ;
And the luſt of my belly can not be told
  For the crisp, gold, delicate fish !

FAN PIECES

1.

MY WHITE untiring wing
Fans scented air
For a young thing,
To make his sighs
Surmise
Of Paradise,
Before he's there.

2.

COOL and light the air I fling to
    The rose-modest girls I kiss.
Sometimes I relent and bring, too,
    Shield for other kisses—this.

3.

I DESIRE pale hands and palaces,
    All inelegance I despise ;
Girls, then ?   No, that's one of your fallacies—
    With cool sleep I kiss his eyes.

FRUITS

Pomegranates.

POLISHED delicates are we,
　Ruby mines in silver earth,
Maiden's blood of high degree
　Curdled into drops of worth,
Breasts of women when they see
　Man is near, and stand them forth.

Figs.

FIGS white, O black, O welcome to my plate,
　White girls of Greece, hot Ethiopian girls,
Though pampered feeders not appreciate,
　So sure of my desire, experienced figs. . .

Wrinkled and young and knowing on high boughs,
　Balanced in every wind and yet rose soft,
More than the blown flower camomile allows
　You wear a wavering scent, honey and sun.

Lemons.

S N O W that takes on saffron,
   Silver turning gold
     Are lemons.
Moons which waver into suns,
   Chrysolite bells and manifold
     Are lemons, lemons.
Camphor ripening to corn light,
   Breasts that else could not be told
     Are lemons, lemons, lemons.

Almonds.

" A s in their sea green shell the pearls,
In triple green we hide, shy girls ;
We care to pass the green of youth
In hauberks bitter and uncouth,
Until the waking comes and we
Wanton white hearts from out our tree."

Small white ones, many in a hand,
Your green down, as I understand,
Is the smooth boyhood of my friend,
And your long halves from end to end
His pretty eyes, O pearls in jade,
Sweet, white, unfaithful, unafraid.

Pears.

HALF acid to a lover's taste,
Flirting hips on a black waist,
Little Ionian,
Little Aleppo,
Little yellow and green girls.

Dates.

WE grow to the sound of the wind
Playing his flutes in our hair,

Palm tree daughters,
Brown flesh Bedouin,
Fed with light
By our gold father ;

We are loved of the free-tented,
The sons of space, the hall-forgetters,
The wide-handed, the bright-sworded
Masters of horses.

Who has rested in the shade of our palms
Shall hear us murmur ever above his sleep.

PLACES

1.

SCENTS rising from the wet earth,
O flowers about Babylon,
Carry a song to my beloved
In that enchanted land
Where her lost kisses starve the world.

2.

I AM Damascus, the heart of bright waters,
They flow silver under my walls
And silver from my walls they flow again.
I am His garden upon earth
And splendour's golden bed ;
There is a blessing upon my terraces,
The souls of those who have known my waters
Sighing upon my terraces.

3.

THE myrtles of Damascus smile and shine
And lift my heart like wine,
        But you . . .
The roses of Baghdad are fed on dew
And moonlight.   Oh, but you,
        If you were mine . . .

4.

GENEROUS is the night in Rabwat valley
Where the flowers give and the breezes carry.
She has a collar of trees and she has rings
Of flowers, and for her the moon brings
Silver to work in the carpet of her fields,
And her birds have silver wings.
One dusk lemon tree her fruit yields
To us drinking at night in Rabwat valley
Where the flowers give and the breezes carry,
Carry.   .   .   .

BIRDS

A Lover Speaks of Them.

1.

WILD pigeon of the leaves,
Brother of lovers,

If you have seen an arrow killing
    From far
The mild-eyed deer
    By rills
    Of summer hills,

If you have heard an arrow singing
   From far
And then strike sheer
    The wings
    Of airy things,

Wild pigeon of the leaves,
   You are
Brother of lovers.

2.

ALLAH has set aside the nightingale
   To be our tears.
    Each prayer for pity
     Which, being dumb, we could not make
   In any ears,
Must agonise, make pale
    His ditty
     For our sake.

Allah has set aside the nightingale
   To be our prayer.
    The nights, which over-long
     Wore down our passion to a burning thread,
He hears not in our tale ;
    And so leans down instead
    To this bird's song
   To find them there.

They Speak for Themselves.

The Swallow.

IF I CHOOSE farmers and their terraces
It is to escape my brothers of the trees ;
The part of stranger is my chief delight ;
The average of the world is not polite
Except to strangers.   I will do no harm
To the provision of my chosen farm,
Neither my building nor my food is theirs ;
These things I gather all from Allah's cares.
It is their wit and not their meat I wish,
Their conversation, not their supper dish,
Their altruistic phrases, not their seed ;
And, as I cost them nothing for my feed,
They learn to love me as a friend indeed.

The Owl.

THEY call me wisdom's fowl, I hear,
But is there wisdom anywhere ?
Wisdom and peace and happiness,
These might be found in loneliness.
Have you a friend, do you see men,
One man ?   You will not find them then.
Even as a drop forecasts the sea
Two souls forecast calamity ;
There are no friends, I thank my God,
In the old wall of my abode.

I doom all sumptuous palaces
To the ill-starred who dwell in these ;
I wish all delicate meats to those
Most poor, whose money golden grows.
Leave me my soul, I've known my soul
In ditch, in wall, in hollow bole,
Potential good, potential ill,
And both still-born and frustrate still.
Nought's to be feared and nought enjoyed
In a void spun upon a void :
Dark speech, and answer dark again ;
Some things are fatal to explain.
Those obligations ?   Very fine,
They forget theirs !   and I with mine ? . . .
They call me wisdom's fowl, I hear,
But is there wisdom anywhere ?

The Falcon.

THAT I am sombre and most spare of words
Is a notorious fact among the birds.
My one perfection and my single beauty
Is taciturn devotion to my duty.
I am not as that fatuous nightingale
Whose ceaseless singing wearies all the vale
And whose intemperate speech, when heard on high,
Brings down misfortune and calamity.
The rule of silence is my one profession,
And my sole virtue lies in my discretion.

When I am caught, I still remain discreet ;
I give no sign that I have felt defeat ;
You will not see my head turned and down cast
To weep above the footsteps of the past,
Rather I look far forward and still chase
The dove of wisdom on from space to space.
So in the end my master yearns to me
And, fearing lest my cold reserve should be
My loss of love, he blinds me with a hood,
(The Koran says : To veil the eyes is good.)
He binds my tongue down to my under beak,
(The Koran says : 'Tis wisdom not to speak.)
He checks my freedom with a silken chain,
(Walk not in pride—the Koran says again.)
Silent and uncomplaining, I abide
These holy bands by which each sense is tied.
My wisdom ripens in the hooded night
Till kings become the servants of my flight ;
Their royal hands bear up my pinions' beat,
I spurn their wrists beneath ascending feet.

The Swan.

M I S T R E S S of each desire, I use the sky,
The water, and the meadow equally ;
With the same calm of confidence I show
My lily-bended neck, my carven snow,
My pouncet box of amber golden-sprent,
My feet of bogwood, in each element.

My royalty is whiteness, loneliness,
And dignity compact ; I am mistress
Of Water's mystery and of the green
Dim glinting drifts of treasure submarine.
While I, self-sailed and with myself for guide,
Grow rich with each adventure of the tide,
The timorous shore-building stay-at-home
Desiring pearls, still nets the bitter foam.

The Crow.

THAT, dressed in black, with harsh importunate cry,
I trouble all delight as I go by ;
That, circling shadow-wise the camps of Spring,
I prophesy their bitter leave-taking ;
That, when I see a love, I croak its doom,
Or, flecking some bright palace with my gloom,
Foretell the speedy ruining of it—
These and more sombre habits I admit.
If you, who blame me for such things, could guess
Wherein lay your abiding happiness,
You would wear midnight garments, even as I,
And curb your conversation to a sigh.
But no ! Vain pleasure is your only goad
And vanity decoys you from the road ;
You cannot realise that friendship is
To blame, not praise, to teach and not to please.
I, only I, of all religious folk,
Retain the symbol of a sable cloak,
And weep for passing time and groan to see
The caravans set out high-heartedly.

All men are deaf.   Although I cry aloud,
They turn their backs upon the morning cloud ;
Alive they will not heed me, though they could,
And dead they cannot hear me, if they would.

Other Wings.

The Bee.

I BUILD my house within the hill,
And, in my feeding, do no ill
Upon the flowers I fasten to
For forage lighter than the dew.
When, with my harmless theft content
And mind on meditation bent,
I go to my abiding place
And brood on bees' predestined grace,
My eye is met at every turn
By works where Euclid deigned to learn.
Of all my musings this is chief :
That toil can be both joy and grief ;
For, if my wax is fruit of pain,
Honey is learning's golden gain.
And next I ponder how my sting
Teaches the whole of love making :
I give all sweet, she gives all sweet
To him who'll take a wound for it.
Love makes all heaviness seem light.
O fools, good-day ! O wise, good-night !

The Moth.

I AM THE lover whose love endlessly
Burns up his heart. Life's and love's law for me
Is to be swift to perish of desire,
Is to count consummation worth the fire.
Her kisses tear the tissue of my wings,
But listen to the song the candle sings :
' Do not condemn me, for I suffer too ;
The flame loves me, even as I love you ;
The sigh of his approach must burn me up,
As he draws near to drink, he melts the cup.
It was by fire that I was driven away
Where I and honey loitered yesterday.
To shed my life, to waste, to weep hot tears,
To jet my little hour to light the years,
Dear moth, dear moth, that is my destiny.'
But fire blazed out to candle and to me :
' You drank my death, eternity was in it.
Have you not lived all living in a minute ? '

DEATH

ONCE he will miss, twice he will miss,
    He only chooses one of many hours ;
For him nor deep nor hill there is,
    But all's one level plain he hunts for flowers.

C

LAMENTS.

Abu Nowas for the Barmacides.

SINCE earth has put you away, O sons of Barmak,
The roads of morning twilight and evening twilight
Are empty.   My heart is empty, O sons of Barmak.

The Wazir Dandan for Prince Sharkan.

WISE to have gone so early to reward,
    Child of the sword ;
Wise with a single new-bathed eagle's flight
    To have touched the white
Wild roses spread for feet in paradise.
    Ah, my son, wise
Soon to have drained the new and bitter cup
    Which, once drunk up,
Leads straightway to an old immortal wine
    Pressed from God's vine.

Her Rival for Aziza.

I PASSED a tomb among green shades
Where seven anemones with down-dropped heads
Wept tears of dew upon the stone beneath.
I questioned underneath my breath
Who the poor dead might be
And a voice answered me. . . .

So now I pray that Allah may be moved
To drop sleep on her eyes because she loved.
She will not care though lovers do not come
To wipe the dust from off a lover's tomb,
She will not care for anything.   But I please
To plant some more dew-wet anemones
    That they may weep.

Haroun Al-Rachid for Heart's-Life.

C H I L D, who went gathering the flowers of death,
My heart's not I, I cannot teach my heart ;
It cries when I forget.
It has not learnt my art
To forget lips when scented with their breath
Or the red cup, when I am drunken yet.

Tumadir Al-Khansa for her Brother.

W E E P ! Weep ! Weep !
These tears are for my brother,
Henceforth that veil which lies between us,
That recent earth,
Shall not be lifted again.

You have gone down to the bitter water
Which all must taste,
And you went pure, saying :
' Life is a buzz of hornets about a lance point.'

STS-C

But my heart remembers, O son of my father and
    mother,
I wither like summer grass,
I shut myself in the tent of consternation.

He is dead, who was the buckler of our tribe
And the foundation of our house,
He has departed in calamity.

He is dead, who was the lighthouse of courageous men,
Who was for the brave
As fires lighted upon the mountains.

He is dead, who rode costly horses,
Shining in his garments.
The hero of the long shoulder belt is dead,
The young man of valiance and beauty breathes no
    more ;
The right hand of generosity is withered,
And the beardless king of our tribe shall breathe no
    more.

He shall be cold beneath his rock.

Say to his mare Alwa
That she must weep
As she runs riderless for ever. . . . .

When the red millstone ground the flowers of youth,
You shattered a thousand horses against the squadrons;
High on the groaning flanks of Alwa
You lifted the bright skirts of your silver mail.

You made the lances live,
You shook their beams,
You quenched their beams in red,
O tiger of the double panoply.

White women wandered with disordered veils
And you saved them in the morning.
Your captives were as troops of antelopes
Whose beauty troubles the first drops of rain. . . .

How effortless were your rhymes of combat
Chanted in tumult, O my brother !
They pierced like lances,
They live among our hearts for ever.

Let the stars go out,
Let the sun withdraw his rays,
He was our star and sun.

Who now will gather in the strangers at dusk
When the sad North whistles with her winds ?
You have laid down and left in the dust, O wanderers,
Him who nourished you with his flocks
And bared his sword for your salvation.
You set him low in the terrible house
Among a few stakes planted,
You threw down boughs of salamah upon him.
He lies among the tombs of our fathers,
Where the days and the years shall pass over him
As they have passed over our fathers.

Your loss is a great distress to me,
Child of the Solamides,
I shall be glad no more. . . .

While you have tears, O daughters of the Solamides,
Weep ! Weep ! Weep !

INSCRIPTIONS AT THE CITY OF BRASS.

I

ENTER and learn the story of the rulers,
They rested a little in the shadow of my towers
And then they passed.
They were dispersed like those shadows
When the sun goes down ;
They were driven like straws
Before the wind of death.

2.

THE drunkenness of youth has passed like a fever,
And yet I saw many things,
Seeing my glory in the days of my glory.
The feet of my war-horse
Drummed upon the cities of the world,
I sacked great towns like a hot wind
And fell like thunder upon far lands.

The kings of the earth were dragged behind my chariot
And the people of the earth behind my laws ;
But now
The drunkenness of youth has passed like a fever,
Like foam upon sand.
Death took me in a net :
My armies warred against him in vain,
My courtiers flattered him in vain.
Listen, O wayfarer, to the words of my death,
For they were not the words of my life :
Save up your soul
And taste the beautiful wine of peace,
For to-morrow the earth shall answer ·
He is with me,
My jealous breast holds him for ever.

3.

ABOUT this table
Sat many hawk-eyed kings
With many one-eyed kings
To bear them company ;
But now all sit in the dark and none are able,
None are able to see.

4.

IN THE name of the Eternal,
In the name of the Master of Strength,
In the name of Him who moves not !
Wayfarer in this place,
Look not upon the glass of appearance,
For a breath may shatter it
And illusion is a pit for the feet of men.

I speak of my power :
I had ten thousand horses
Groomed by captive kings,
I had a thousand virgins of royal blood
To serve my pleasure
And a thousand excellent virgins
With moon-coloured breasts,
Chosen from all the world.
They brought forth little princes in my chambers
And the little princes were as brave as lions.
I had peculiar treasures
And the West and the East were two heads
Bowing before me.
I thought my power eternal
And the days of my life
Fixed surely in the years ;
But a whisper came to me
From Him who dies not.
I called my captains and my strong riders,
Thousands upon thousands
With swords and lances ;
I called my tributary kings together
And those who were proud rulers under me,
I opened the boxes of my treasure to them, saying :
' Take hills of gold, mountains of silver,
And give me one more day upon the earth.'
But they stood silent,
Looking upon the ground ;
So that I died
And death came to sit upon my throne.
I was Kush bin Shadad bin Ad,
Surnamed the Great.

5.

O SONS of men,
You add the future to the future
But your sum is spoiled
By the grey cypher of death.
There is a Master
Who breathes upon armies,
Building a narrow and dark house for kings.
These wake above their dust
In a black commonwealth.

6.

O SONS of men,
Why do you put your hands before your eyes
And play in this road as if for ever,
Which is a short passing to another place ?
Where are the kings
Whose loins jetted empires,
Where are the very strong men,
Masters of Irak ?
Where are the lords of Ispahan,
O sons of men ?

7.

O SONS of men,
You see a stranger upon the road,
You call to him and he does not stop.

He is your life
Walking towards time,
Hurrying to meet the kings of India and China,
Hurrying to greet the sultans of Sina and Nubia,
Who were blown over the mountain crest
By a certain breath,
Even as he.

8.

O SONS of men,
Lean death perches upon your shoulder
Looking down into your cup of wine,
Looking down on the breasts of your lady.
You are caught in the web of the world
And the spider Nothing waits behind it.
Where are the men with towering hopes ?
They have changed places with owls,
Owls who lived in tombs
And now inhabit a palace.

TRADES AND CRIES.

I.

ALL TRADES are jewels in the crown of state,
    But one round pearl of price the centre harbours,
Which to themselves each guild would arrogate ;
    While I have always said it was the barber's,
Who stands with subtle steel and phrases bland,
Holding the heads of kings beneath his hand.

2.

HERE'S cool water for you,
Here's fresh water !
Crystal light, my water,
Joy of throats, my water,
Diamonds, my water !

3.

O YOU who go with heavy bales
Beneath a press of sounding sails,
    Pity the fisher by his nets at sea :
Under a night of stars
Weary and worn he wars,
    That you may eat your fish in luxury.

Night-long he sees the heaving breasts
Of his nets on the water crests
    And never any other breast sees he ;
While you wake with the day
Beside a sleeping may
    Whose breasts are like the sun upon the sea.

Yet my laborious nights and days
Are consecrated to His praise
    Who gives each man a station carefully ;
By Whose eternal wish
Ther're some to eat the fish
    And some to catch them in the nets at sea.

4.

GLASSES, glasses,
Blown drops of the sunrise,
Breasts of alabaster little girls,
Frozen breath of virgins under desire,
Eye-coloured of the fairest ;
Navels of small sweethearts,
Hardened spun honey ;
Glasses, glasses !

LUTES.

1.

I WAS THE green branch of a tree
Birds loved and taught their songs to.
Haply the teaching lingers,
For, when I lie on beauty's knee,
Remember under beauty's fingers,
The woodland song I sing belongs to
The birds who sang to me.

2.

I WAS A green branch of nightingales,
And, while they taught me music in gold nights,
I dared not stir my leaves.
Now, a fragile lute which grieves
Beneath the touch of tiny nails,

Now, clasped by slim delights
And lying on young breasts,
Remembering my nightingales
I bring a woodland bliss
To lovers' feasts
And spill wine's ecstasy where no wine is.

3.

PLAYER upon the Persian lute, your hands
Calm and exalt and follow your commands
Even as a doctor, feeling with his skill,
Makes the hot life-blood hasten or be still.
Player upon the Persian lute, your fine
And foreign fingers the sweet cords combine
Until each hears his native song, and each
Who does not know, yet understands your speech

FLOWERS

HOW sad-coloured the earth would seem,
How grey each water stream,
If flowers were dead.
God said :
Let there be flowers,
Let streams be filled with showers ;
And then decreed my lazy hours
Should pass in water-meadows filled with flowers.

Roses.

YOU HIDE your crimson blushets in green sleeves,
Balmed hearts of all slight crystal, riders in rose
Who lead the coloured armies of the flowers ;

Sweeter you open shameless to the breeze
Than kissed wine on child mouths.

                                        Your rainbow blood
Riotously compares you with gold dawn,
With cups of purple wine, with garnet fruit
On emerald branches, O silver-quivered
Desirous roses ; and you chain your loves
With different-tinted coquetry of robes
So that they do not tire. . . .

The Song of the Rose.

MY VISIT is shorter than a ghost's,
Between Winter, it is, and Summer.
Hasten to play with me, play with me ;
Time is a sword.

I balm my breath,
I am the colour of love,
I tingle in the hand of the girl who takes me.
I am your guest,
Hope not to keep me long,
The nightingale loves me.

I am the glory,
But the glory is hardest pressed of all the flowers.
I am the ever wounded,
Thorns spring out on my youth,
Steel arrows splashing my silks with my blood,
Staining my silks vermilion.

Yet I remain the elegant of passing things,
The pride of morning.
I wear my beauty in a crystal shift of dew.

Men hurry me from my green to another crystal,
My body turns to water, my heart is burned,
My tears are collected
And my flesh is torn.
I feel the passion of fire,
My soul is fumed off,
My spirit goes in vapour ;
My sweet sweat is a record of my pain.
The passionate
Breathe the musk of my cast garments with delight ;
My body goes from you, but my soul remains ;
The wise do not regret my little time in the garden,
But lovers would have me,
Silly pretty lovers,
Have me there for ever.

The Song of the Jasmin.

C O M E to me and mourn not, I am the jasmin.
My stars are whiter than silver
On the blue noon of air.

I come from the breast of God
To the breasts of women,
And am an ornament for black hair.

Use wine with me
And your friend's laughter
Shall shine more white.

My tint attests the camphor ;
I am here when I am not here
So sweet am I.

My name detects the error of despair,
I am white joy, my lords.

The Song of the Narcissus.

M Y B E A U T Y is not wine to me,
For I have eyes of languor,
And balance like music
And am nobly born.

I consider the flowers,
I talk with the flowers in moonlight.
My beauty gives me a throne among them,
Yet I am a slave.

I am a slave,
The cincture of obedience,
The good servant
Who stands with a straight body
And bowed head.

I bare my neck,
I abide in my pure tent
Pitched on an emerald column ;
My robe is gold and silver.

My modesty will excuse the wantoning of my eyes
As I hang my head above the waters.

The Song of the Violet.

I WEAR a green cymar,
A sea-purple robe of honour,
Being quite little
And delightful.

My sister the rose is the pride of morning,
And I am the mystery of morning,
I am the dark child
Who wears an early grief.

You would have thought the modesty of my short
     hours . . .

I ravish my darlings for half a day,
And they pull me and use me and sell me cheap,
Make songs about me
And then despise me.

But in the morning the wise lift me
From my pale drought of death,
And balm disease with me.

The scent of my small life delighted the lad,
And my body dies for him.

But, but,
A little army with purple shields,
With emerald helmets,
Riding to victory . . .

The Song of the Nenuphar.

MY SHAME could not live naked in the air,
I chose the passion of the water ;
Immaculate petals
Guessed at rather than seen.
(Lovers, remember this !)
The river places are the bed of my rest
For ever.

That I should thirst
When he has given me to drink
Is love.
I thrust my gold cup to the sun
But night on the waters
Draws me as the moon draws
The waters.

I take my dreams to the green nest of water.

You lose me ?
I am carried with open eyes ;
We die together, water and I,
And you say you lose me.

He gave me what I am,
My shame could not live naked in the air,
I chose the passion of the water ;
Immaculate petals
Guessed at rather than seen.

The Song of the Gillyflower.

THE YELLOW garment of love sickness,
The white and yearning robe,
The blue frustrated veil . . .

I am a wise white, He knows,
For they will not touch my unscented nakedness.

STS-D

And I am a wise yellow, Allah knows,
For I blab the scent of my secret,
But not your secret.

Also I am a grief-bound blue
For light offends my mystery.

I break at night, He knows !

The Song of the Camomile.

SYMBOLISTS, symbolists . . .
And, if not, sleep . . .

Have you seen my flowers spreading on the fields,
The far-noticed white,
And the yellow disk giving languor ?
The verses of the Book,
And the difficult verses ?

You have come to me and delighted,
You have come to me again and lo ! I was not.
And you have not understood.

My bruised soul
Mounts into the singing of the doves
And you have thought it pleasure ;
Though my white is recognisable far off,
You lie in the fields of my painting
And have not understood.

The Song of the Lavender.

I AM no terrace flower,
Vile hands and foolish talk
Escape me,
I grow in the hot brown dust,
Loving not men, but man.

No slave, no city thing
Can touch me.
Come to me in the waste heart of Arabia
Far from the dwellings of pale men,
For my delight is there.

I am the mistress of hermits,
Wild bees, deer, and the bitter absinthe
Are my sisters,
I am a free girl knowing no market.
Lust seeks me not, but the wild rider
Seeks me.

I would wish you to come to the valleys
Where the breeze kisses me at morning,
I would wish you
To lie near the wine of me.

Allah, Allah,
Even the camel-boy, telling of me,
Forgets his oaths !

The Song of the Anemone.

I F M Y heart were as my body,
I should be above
The crying of the coloured flowers.

For his girl's cheek
A lover carries my blood as a flask of praise.

Yet the vases of the feast do not invite me
Because my heart is black.

I will fight no more.

I am the bright still of unhappiness.

WINE

For E. Allen Ashwin.

I.

GRAPES big with wine, are you more sweet
Black-coated like the crow
Yet twinkling in the sombre vine
As henna-painted fingers shine
When China queens sit all a-row
With folded saffron feet,

Or pressed to drunken honey in the vats?

2.

P O U R that old wine for me
And for my friend, this child.
It is a precious wine
Spilled for a wine-adept.
I cannot find a name
For its mild flame
Except :
Wine of my friend, this child.

3.

L E T T H E small cup and the deep cup go round,
Old friends, begin !
Take little cups from little hands
Whose camphor tips are fairy-lands,
But wait, to suck the mighty in,
For the lute's sound.

4.

S O M E W I S E electuary or balm,
   Some learned knife,
     May cure particular complaints ;
     But when the whole soul faints
Here is the old, the calm,
   The purple remedy for life.

5.

THERE'S NOTHING like the blood of grapes
To give escapes
From care's infesting, festering apes.
To set the wit upon probation,
To give an edge to conversation,
To make a friend of a relation,
There's nothing like the blood of grapes.

6.

O NIGHT, O eyes of love,

Never drink without a song,
Grooms who take a horse to water
Whistle it along.

O night, O eyes of love !

Never, never drink at all
Save with girls to make your passion
Great as they are small.

O night, O eyes of love !

7.

NEVER TAKE wine except from a blithe boy,
    For, if you hold him to you while you sup,
His cheeks' reflection strengthens the red joy
    And more than roses blossom in the cup.

8.

O N   T H I S preferred and easy night
  The cup was never empty of its red ;
I said to sleep : ' We know you not,' and said :
  ' I know you,' to her thighs of silver white.

9.

I D O L carved by Chinese hands
From a wild-rose, leave your lazy
Lazy couching, eyes of jade.
Pour me out the young undying
Tulip-coloured wine from Chinese places.

Pour it laughing to the cup,
Laughing in the lips of folly,
Yet as pure as your boy's heart ;
I will set my mouth to drinking,
Sucking blood from the black throats of wineskins.

Tell a man who was born drunk
Wine's betraying ? Never do so.
(As the curling of your hair
My desires are complicated.)
Bad for poets ? While the sky's blue tunic

Hangs at the green door of earth ?
I will drown myself in wine baths ;
When they smell the scarlet rose
From my heart below the meadow,
Pretty weeping boys shall laugh home reeling.

10.

THERE'S death in wine,
White hands woo out from the green sleeves,
There's death in wine, there's death to care,
White hands win out from the green leaves,
A web of drows'd forgetting the violet weaves,
And the narcissus has a Lethe'd hair,
And there are girls.

HOUSES AND HOSPITALITY.

1.

SO SLIGHT and gold the stone that the house seems
Gilded with flame upon a base of dreams.

2.

HOUSE, haunted with bird music,
Of proud thresholds,

Sobbing with desire came the lover,
    Your doors were wide for him ;
We looked in gladness to discover
    Your hidden bride for him.

Chamberlains of luxurious lot
    Grew ruddy there;
    Brocade was everywhere,
House, haunted with bird music,
But she was not.

3.

A STRANGER building in a stranger land
    Lays his foundation on the fickle air;
Against a breeze his palace may not stand
    And the first puff of wind will leave him bare.

4.

OUR HOUSE shall have a narrow door
    That grief and time may not come in,
    But friends and laughter, who were thin,
Shall enter, fatten, leave no more.

5.

MAY THIS house rise in air
As long as birds chant in its garden blooms,
And friendship scent its rooms
As long as flowers die of being fair.

As long as new stars come in spring to browse
The meadows of the sky,
As long as fruits on trees are born and die,
Live all who use this house.

6.

O VISITOR, O wine upon our hearts
   Making them dance, we laugh and live to-day,
   We blossom in the warm benignant ray
Which is our guest; we die if he departs.

7.

IF WE had known, prince of urbanities,
   We would have made our welcoming more sweet
   And spread our heart's red carpet for your feet
And spread the soft black velvet of our eyes.

8.

THEY came: our hills put on their green
And the yellow flower of the sun to bloom again.
' Ah, good-bye pain,
For frost is dead
And the first violet seen,'
We said.

WARRIORS

1.

H I S I N K was blood and his good lance at rest
    A ready pen
    For fair caligraphy ;
It wrote red songs in praise of victory
Upon the white papyrus of the breast
    Of other men.

2

T H E knights came to me,
They bade me defiance ;
    Ungird me now.

They wished to take me,
They looked for compliance ;
    Ungird me now.

I fed them all
To my brothers, the lions ;
    Ungird me now.

3

I C A L L sweet pasture for my blade
Because he never bade retreat,
    Retreat, retreat, retreat ;
      Ride if you dare !

I call your heads to the red sand,
Your hearts to vultures and to crows,
    To crows, to crows, to crows ;
        Ride if you dare !

I call my sword a cup-bearer
Because he pours a cheer of myrrh,
    Of myrrh, of myrrh, of myrrh ;
        Ride if you dare !

I call for my grief's bitter bath,
My feet tread out a path of blood
    Like myrrh ! The crows retreat ;
        Ride if you dare !

                    4.

H A V E you not seen, O eyeless head,
    Your brothers welter in their clots,
    And how the Vulture's breathing blots
The scarlet from the cheeks of dread ?

Did you hope lessons from my wrath,
    Or any teaching from my frowns
    Save how a lance-head flourish drowns
Dead kidneys in a crow-black bath ?

5.

THE DAUGHTERS OF THE POET FIND.

*When the battle was doubtful, they stripped themselves
naked, save for their green bracelets and anklets, and,
each running to the front of one wing, heartened their father's
men with these improvisations.*

Ofairah the Suns.

R E D swords, children of Bekr! Red swords!
Heat the battle red, O sons of Zimman!
The heights are drowned in horses,
Heat the battle red!

Put on red robes of honour
And our arms shall be white for you,
Lay on red swords this morning, sons of Bekr!

Let your wounds be wide as the rent garment
Of a mad mistress,
And we will prepare our bodies for you
On soft cushions.
Let your swords be red!

Red swords, red roses, sons of Bekr!
Children of Zimman, heat the battle red!

Hozaylah the Moons.

CARVE all, carve all, O children of Zimman,
Carve with your cutting swords!
Shake down the red thunderbolts,
O sons of Bekr!

We are the daughters of the morning star
Nard-haired,
Pearls are about us . . .
Shake down the red thunderbolts, O riders,
And we are yours!

Mow us a red carpet for our feet,
O riders of Rabiah!
Hozaylah of Moons is for the reddest sword!

6

PSALM OF BATTLE.

GOD IS praise and glory;
Therefore glory and praise be unto Him
Who led me by the hand in stony places,
Who gave me a treasure of gold and a throne of gold
And set a sword of victory in my hand!

He covered the earth with the shadow of my kingdom,
And fed me when I was a stranger
Among strange peoples;
When I was lowly He accounted me
And He has bound my brow about with triumph.

His enemies fled before my face like cattle;
The Lord breathed upon them and they were not!

Not with the ferment of a generous wine
But with death's evil grape
He has sent them drunken into the darkness.

We died, we died in the battle,
But He has set us upon happy grass
Beside an eternal river of scented honey.

BREEZES AND GARDENS.

I.

WOULD you have gardens, come to me . . .
The breeze, the perfumed vagabond,
False to all else, is true to me
And he shall heal your misery.
The flowers give coloured robes to me
And laugh with all their petalled sleeves,
And they shall heal your misery.
The wet sky gives an alms to me,
Gaudily bending down my trees ;
My fruit shall heal your misery.
The Seven Stars drop gifts to me
Of watered gold and cloudy pearl,
And Zephyr fans the gold for me ;
My night shall heal your misery.
The loves of dawn are swift with me
To lie upon my eager streams
And kiss the sleeping flowers for me. . . .
Shall I not heal your misery ?

2.

M Y song
Of coloured music
Overlaid with gold
Has chanted and extolled
The power of bitterness
A thought too long.

My themes are these,
If so you please :

Dark-glancing deer that tread a garden of roses,
Where bees bring honey and the dawn weeps her dew
To fashion breasts like summer-dreaming pears.
The wind stirs in the branches of the women
Pure as unthreaded pearls ;
I smell the flower-essences upon them
To sunset flutes
And wine drunk out on the narcissus lawns.
Water of red lips to be drunk
Beside garden streams :

These are my themes.

My song
Of coloured music
Overlaid with gold
Has chanted and extolled
The power of bitterness
A thought too long.

3.

I KNOW by his scent
Before he reaches my hair
That the breeze has risen and dances upon the meadow.

If one could take love as one takes a lover
And rest his head between the breasts
And know peace !

These green and gold and blue toys
Which Allah calls his world,
How can I play with them without Aziz ?

4

YOU WALK in the garth and piqued roses adore you,
Dropping their dry and coloured leaves before you ;
The silver lilies close their eyelids, while
The scented camomile
And other red flowers dare not smile.
When, fairest, when
Shall the two dusty violets of my mouth
Attain their cyclamen
And slake their drouth ?
The lavender has said : ' Be apposite,
O moon of white,
But for one night ! '

5.

The Song of the Light Breeze.

I COME up out of the south in autumn time
To fill my fruits, my coloured loves
For prime.
My winter fingers from the west are doves
Whose grey wings free the branches, whose fans give
Dry healing that the tree may live.

At morn
I carry the scent,
I make flowers speak with flowers, I balance the corn,
I give the streams their silver chain,
I quick the palm, and lead lost youth again
Back to a woman's tent.

DISPRAISE.

Of Eloquence.

BEWARE the sweet before the fox has sprung,
The fox behind the honey of his tongue.

Of Judges.

THEY sat on a high seat
    And snipped the robe of Justice by the hem
But now they lie with folded feet
    And the worms out-argue them.

Of Beards.

HE HAD a mighty beard to left and right . . .
She was as sad as a cold winter night.

Of Time.

TIME has undone
    My body's quickness
        Ruthlessly :
Once I was straight and walked towards the sun,
    But now I keep the house with my friend, Sickness,
        And my last mistress, Immobility.

Of Misers.

NO SOONER had I come to visit these,
    Than all the house, wife, husband, son, and daughter,
Ran out behind and hid among the trees
    For fear I'd ask them for a cup of water.

Of Old Men.

I PRAYED to kiss her scarlet mouth ;
    She did not take offence,
    But only showed indifference.
The corner of her scarlet mouth
    Dropped this sole answer to my prayer :
    ' I do not love white hair
Or wet white cotton in my scarlet mouth.'

Of Woman.

1.

YOU ASK me about women, I reply:
' Look at this wagging lip, this sunken eye
     The early white upon this scanty hair,
The rot of this strong body which was I.'

2.

WOMAN: that is to say
A body which the birds of prey
Disdain to take away.

Woman: the word implies
A thing which lies
With you at night, about you at sunrise.

3.

HOPELESS at night I squirm
Beside the rough-legged worm
     I call my wife.
On that dark funeral day
When we were wedded, say
     Where was my knife?
Where the cold poison cup
For her to tipple up
     And sneeze out life?

Of This World.

THE picture of this world for all to see
Is painted on both sides ? That well may be.
    Hypocrisy and lies are on the front
And on the back, lies and hypocrisy.

WISDOM AND CONDUCT.

For Tom Staveley.

1.

MY GOLD is lost, my life is spared ;
    That is to say
My finger nails are pared,
    A thing of every day.

2.

IN LIFE of time two rivers join,
    One muddy and one clear ;
Two days in time of life there are,
    The soft and the severe ;
You may trust time and life as far
As you would trust the spinning of a coin,
    Or very near.

3

SCAN Noble's lineage and you will find
Age after age a Noble of that kind :
Vile's line is just as long, for, all the while,
Vile's father's father's father's name was Vile.

4.

AS THE sun yellows before setting,
So man, who sinks to his forgetting,
    Shines in his dying ;
And as the death-struck bird sings loudest,
So a man's soul is puffed and proudest
    Poised for its flying.

5.

THE wise man hatches out a plan
    By sitting on it like a hen ;
The cautious and inactive man
    Is blessed above all other men.

6.

In Prison.

FOOLS take the prize
    And cruelty lives on,
While wisdom dies
    And kindness is undone.
If I come free
    I'll swear to change my ways,
And practise ignorance and cruelty
    Through all my days.

7.

THE LAST place where a helper shall be found
　Is in that quarter whence the danger came ;
　You would not treat a scalded hand with flame,
Or give a cup of water to the drowned.

8.

THERE are hidden streams whose courses
　No one forces,
Places hidden in the snows
　No one knows,
Pastured stars whose silver beaches
　No one reaches. . . .
And the black crows make a tomb,
　Fifty flying graves of gloom,
　　To engulf no matter whom.

9.

INK IS the strongest Drug that God has made ;
If you can write of Beauty unafraid,
　You will be praising Him who gave the Ink
More than all Prayers unlearned men have prayed.

10.

I HAVE nothing, nothing,
And my heart is light ;
A rag for clothing,
No wife for loathing,
Coarse salt for soothing
Bread or dough thing,
And then nothing—
Do you wonder my heart is light ?

11.

THOSE who abused my open hand of old,
    Now it is closed are still abusing it.
I have made enemies in making gold,
    But many more by losing it.

12.

WHAT'S danger, so the feet may roam
    Beyond the town where custom is ?
Better be dead than stay at home,
    A flea with lice for enemies . . .
    Invite your soul to voyages,
For at the gates of new found lands
    Wait raptures and discoveries
And gold with laughter in her hands.

13.

WHEN two young lovers fair and fit
　Kiss each the other's soul into eclipse,
Not they, but He who made their lips
　Shall answer it.

14.

POOR silly heart,
You think a kiss is deathless ;
Do you not see eclipse
Standing a little apart,
Breathless,
Finger to lips ?

15.

　WHEN things fall odd,
Sit down in peace and send your cares to Satan.
If life's a tangle much too big to straighten,
　Give it to God.

16.

I LEAVE this garden with a blood-red tulip
　Deep in my heart for wound and ornament.
Unhappy he, who from a greater garden
Were called with no flower in his tunic fold,
　Nor time to gather one before he went.

17.

PRAISE be to Him whose deep design
Has made your fortune equal mine ;
His poor are rich in smiles, and see
His rich are poor in gaiety.

18.

WHAT is success ?
The deathless daughter
Of your weariness.
It is to dive in deeper, deeper water,
And even deeper, layer on layer
Of cold green mystery,
For an ever rosier, ever whiter, ever greyer
Pearl of the sea.

19.

LET TIME do what it will,
I shall do ill.

20.

GREEN girls think men are all alike
    Because each wears a turban ;
But one will be a country tyke
    And one a knowing urban,
One be a white and kindling star,
    One murky, lacking culture ;
One a clean feed, as eagles are,
    And one a corpse-fed vulture.

21.

B E N O T astonished that the golden wind
Blows the world forward, leaving you behind ;
   There are no dinars in a rose-wood pen
For any but a merchant's hand to find.

22.

S I N G the joys of vagabonding,
All that's beautiful travels far ;
Even the moon-coloured pearl
Must forsake the deep green levels,
Leave the ancient ocean's bonding,
And be drawn across the beaches
Where the waiting merchants are,
Ere it shows and glows and reaches
To a crown's immortal bevels
Or the white neck of a girl.

23.

Advice to Mendicant Women.

I F Y O U would beg, plain nakedness is best,
   A leg's a better beggar than all wailing,
For there is no investment in a vest,
   And only to be veiled is unavailing.

24.

O L D hollow trees
Look gay with murmuring multitudes of bees
And golden droppings of the combs' increase ;
But when the honey's drained and dead
And all the bees have fled,
Remains this sorry sight inStead :
Old hollow trees.

25.

I F E E D my soul with crumbled hopes
　　Until the rocks die down like snow,
　　For patience has more power, I know,
Than fifty gilded horoscopes.

26.

T H E Y said :
Your cultured head
Shines on the black
Of learning's lack
In other men.

Pray cease,
(I answered then,)
My girth's increase
And daily peace
Would be maintained
More by the earning
Of a harlot's hour,
Than by the power
Of all my learning.

My books and ink
With all I know and think,
In this world's mart
Would kick the beam
Against a salted bream
And a stale tart.

27.

W H O beauty loveth and created hath
With the same breath which bade us fear Thy wrath,
   Lover and Lord, we pray Thee to remove
Either restraint or beauty from our path.

28.

S U R E L Y it is a pleasant thing
   To fill the mouths of friends with golden gifts.
   (Only beware the shifts
Of fortune's wing.)

The drowsy nights are sent to steep
   The over-laboured senses of the day.
   (But of what use are they
If she'll not sleep ?)

29.

T H E R E are two beings you may not offend :
God and a friend.

30.

PULL up the roots of your soul and flee away;
  Torn and in exile she is better
  Than held in fetter
On her native clay.

God spreads the vast of His carpet for your feet
  Woven of rainy hills and valleys,
  Gardens and alleys
Lilied and complete.

31.

IF YOU would know the taste of bitterness
Seek sorrow out and comfort her distress;
You need not feed a jackal cub to see
Just how ungrateful gratitude can be.

32.

GOD writes for eternity, this is not given to men;
But even He cannot rewrite it again,
And we walk in the wake of His pen.

We have followed the tracing of the letters of God, my
      friend,
The outline was not ours to mar or to mend;
Sit quiet and wait for the end.

WAYS OF LOVE.

For Alec Robertson.

1.

RISE up and hear the season sing,
The girls are here for marrying,
And a glad wife's an almanac
Whose scented leaves point ever back
And tell about the Spring.

2.

OUR BED is silver hung with sea yellow
But fairer is my bed-fellow
Than it, or anything the sky below.

3.

'SYRUP of roses, ice, and stay in bed,'
    Said the doctor who came
    To physic my flame.
'Bring me her cheeks, her heart, herself,' I said.

4.

LOVE was before the light began,
When light is over, love shall be;
O warm hand in the grave, O bridge of truth,
O ivy's tooth
Eating the green heart of the tree
Of man !

5.

WITH black glances
And haughty poses
Of her white slimness
(Bow down, lances
Famed for straightness!)
She proposes
Now to flout me
For my lateness
And advances—
Starlit-dimness
Of wet roses
Grows about me.

When as now
Her tumbled hair
Falls adorning
A clear brow,
(Who has seen the phœnix nesting
On an aromatic bosom
Woven of the sweet and rare
Branches of his fabled gum-tree ?)

Lo, the night's black wing is resting
On the blossom
Of the plum-tree
Of the morning.

6.

W H O sings your slender body is a reed,
    His simile a little misses ;
Reeds must be naked to be fair indeed,
    While your sweet garments are but added blisses.

Who sings your body is a slender bough
    Also commits a kindred folly ;
Boughs to be fair must have green leaves enow
    And you, my white one, must be naked wholly.

7.

    M Y sickness is love-lack ;
O doctor, do not probe and ask,
    But give her back,
Who is a silver salve in a gold flask.

8.

A N arrow's hum,
Surprise,
A wound, abasement !
Bowmen
Or eyes ?
Or did it come
From foemen
Or a casement ?

9.

S L E E P E R, the palm-trees drink the breathless noon,
A golden bee sucks at a fainting rose,
Your lips smile in their sleep.   Oh, do not move.

Sleeper, oh, do not move the gilded gauze
Which lies about your gold, or you will scare
The sun's gold fire which leaps within your cryStal.

Sleeper, oh, do not move ; your breaSts in sleep,
Allah, they dip and fall like waves at sea ;
Your breaSts are snow, I breathe them like sea foam,
I taSte them like white salt.   They dip and fall.

Sleeper, they dip and fall.   The smiling Stream
Stifles its laugh, the gold bee on the leaf
Dies of much love and rosy drunkenness,
My eyes burn the red grapes upon your breaSts.

Sleeper, oh, let them burn, let my heart's flower,
Fed on the rose and santal of your fleSh,
BurSt like a poppy in this solitude,
In this cool silence.

10.

I W E A R I E D of my friend and of the EaSt,
    At morn I journeyed to the novel WeSt ;
I found an unknown savour in the feaSt
    And in the casual wine an unknown zeSt,
(That day's firSt dusk had led me back to EaSt
    And I had lain all night upon his breaSt).

11.

TO LIGHTEN my darkness,
I look for the red crescent of her lips
And if that comes not
I look for the blue crescent
Of the sword of death.

Oh, joy of friends gathered upon the cool meadow
To drink wine handed by white hands !

Flowers of Spring on the meadow
Between spread slim fingers !

You sit drinking the tulip-coloured wine
In the midst of this green earth
With all her waters.

12.

HER belly's concord can make slaves,
    Her waist might take for its device
The thin green flag the willow waves
    Or ' As the poplars grow in paradise.'

There is wild honey on her lips,
    She drinks and sweetens all the wine ;
Two stars have gone to their eclipse
    When her bold eyes leap wanton into mine.

13.

T I M E, where are the old hours in whose gold mirth
I lay with love upon adored earth ?

Time has put by the coloured days of laughter
And all the smiling nights which followed after.

Time has gnawed thin the pillow of my reſt.
Who evilly worked where I had loved the beſt ?
Time !

14.

Y O U R skin is snow,
Your henna is wet-black ſtill,
As your fingers and palms will
Show.

It would pass all skill
To render so
On so small a page
A black bird in an ivory cage.

15.

I L O V E a fawn with eyes of languishment ;
If you would know the foreſt way he went,
   Watch what young branches ſtill are practiſing
Their juſt-learned lesson of the way he bent.

16.

Inscription on a Chemise.

N O H A N D has been allowed to touch
 The rose I hide,
  Though eyes have looked upon it and desired it.
   Surely the thought of all this foiled desire
   Should feed your fire
 And fan your pride
And raise the value of the bud, as such,
  If it required it !

17.

T H E B R E E Z E of his coming
Plays on the sand of my heart.

O night beside him !
O tired lips leeching wine,
Achieving honey,
Knowing at last Spring !

18.

T H E N I G H T is witch-blown glass of blue,
Out of a green mystery the nightingale
Invites us ;

The breathing of the naked night
Into the silver horn of the moon
Invites us ;

Suspicious age is sleeping ;

Here are myrtles and gold flowers,
The roses' jars are spilled
And wine and stars ;

The cup is full to-night.

19.

K N O W you the surliest
Heart hid away from you,
Parted away from you,
Lies broken-hearted ?
And mine with the earliest ?

Know you how many
Slaughters your eyes have made,
Daughters your eyes have made
Waver as waters ?
And I before any ?

20.

F A R F R O M the eyes which the narcissus loves
Cast not my heart ;
Mock not the the crying of the drunkards,
Lead them back to the tavern.

The armies of his boy's beard
Compass my heart,
And, as a wounded rose,
The rent in my robe shall not be sewn.

O brown tyrannous beauty,
My heart lies at your feet of jasmin,
My heart of a little girl at your thief's feet.

21.

I s a w not love, my eyes were closed, a dart
    In by my ear made he.
I do not know what has passed between some lady
    And my heart.

22.

H e r body is silk like water,
With the curves of water,
Pure and restful as water.

To be with her in the night !
Her hair, the wings of night ;
And her hands the pale stars of night.

God said : Let there be eyes,
And lo ! the dew of her eyes,
The dark wine of her eyes.

23.

A THIEF of hearts, equipped with all bright imple
    ments,
    With nard of gardens in her curls of hair,
    With lips of ruby-sugared condiments
    And in her cheek musk rose of gardens too,
    And teeth like cryStal when the sun is bare,
A thief of hearts, equipped with all bright implements
    For breaking through.

24.

BLACK eyes with blue kohl length,
    White breaSts with red coal tips,
Wine-coloured lips with honey Strength,
    A happiness of hips,
        Black night where grope
        The lips of hope
    Towards a white eclipse.

25.

YOU WHO have fought not, have not taken scars,
Would feed your appetite,
As if it were a thing of every night
To reach the Stars.

26.

Ten Girls on a Meadow.

T H E M O O N shines and the grasses shine
With candid girls and argentine,
The grasses sigh and shine.

Those slimly dancing bodies wave
With the same sway that green reeds have,
Or as the grasses wave.

Ah, vine-borne clusters of new grapes,
So the hair falls down on their napes,
Like yellow grapes and purple grapes.

As long brown arrows dipped in gold
Their eye-glances ; the shots are told
And my heart is the gold.

27.

O N C E , when I looked, his glance unto my glance
        Was parallel always,
But now I look upon an angle of his gaze,
        Oh, lance, oh, lance !

28.

M U S K kisses,
To faint under musk,
To feel his body bend like a wet branch
That has eaten of the west wind and drunk dew.

Musk kisses,
To madden without wine :
Should I not know, who get drunk each sunset
With the musk, musk, musk wine of his mouth ?

Musk kisses,
Beauty looked into his mirror at morning
And turned from her own shadow
To love the musk, musk, musk of his nakedness.

29.

Inscription on a Chemise.

THREE things alone
Prevent her black eyes saying yes :
Fear of the unknown and horror of the known
    And her own loveliness.

30.

YOU ARE that hind which led the lions in
    Made tame by your black bow,
        Egyptian girl.

Your tented dim silk hair has fallen low
    And you are couched therein,
        Egyptian girl.

Crystal grows grey, and the blue airs begin
  To hide their shame in snow,
      Egyptian girl.

You hide your roses with your hand, but lo !
  We see the hand, we sin,
      Egyptian girl.

31.

THE WATER-WHEELS, which weep from either
    eye
  Yet make a merry chanting as they spin,
Are like young lovers who will groan and cry
  When all their heart is ecstasy within.

32.

Embroidered on a Handkerchief.

HERE I MY secret heart have stripped
In slight elaborated script ;
If you object : ' It is indeed
Too tortured and too fine to read,'
I answer : ' Nothing is too fine
To symbolise this love of mine,
And lines of complicated art
Are no more tortured than my heart.'

33.

THERE IS no corner of his body negligible,
Surely his eyes have fired the houses of this city ;
He has black scorpion curls
And tender limbs of silver silk,
He's wild and witty ;
The steel light of his smile is not to tell,
And his backside will shake like curdled milk,
Poor girls.

34.

MOURNFUL numbers played on my heart-strings,
    Played by grief :
    Night, the thief,
Night will tell you of these things.

Sleepless shepherds counting every star
    Are my eyes :
    Night, the wise,
Night will tell you that they are.

35.

Up at a Window.

AMAZEMENT, amazement,
A moon has risen in a little dusk,
A Mars of lips
In one small casement,
A rose in an eclipse
Of musk !

36.

Y O U walk as proudly as a pirate ship
Walks on the sea, you have a falcon's eyes,
Your hair is a black youth sold with white girls,
Your words are scarlet dyes,
You wear your silver beauty as a belt
Which will not slip
For any speech,
You will not melt
For gold
Or for my soul
Or for my sleep
Or for my eyes,
O roses set too high for man to reach.

37.

I S E E in my heart
Clouds and lights dart,
Part quicksilver, part
  Blood on the sea.
When the night has gone
We shall be joined anon
Like river and swan,
  I and she.

38.

M Y love is a young thing, she gives me wine
With bread of gaiety, and she is mine.
She is a garden with fountains, the twin still
Waters her eyes, her voice the silver rill.

39.

" *When he had made an end of this song, my master gave
a great sigh of happiness and, leaning his head upon his
breast, seemed to sleep. The girl slipped from his arms,
fearing to trouble his repose, and glided from my presence.
I went to cover my companion and prop his head with a
cushion ; but I saw that he had ceased to breathe. I
leaned anxiously over him, and discovered that he had died
smiling at life, like those who are born under a happy star.
Allah be good to him !* "

I AM red wise
For wine is more than roses,
Water's for prayers ;
Your cheeks run wine,
My soul reels and runs crimson wisdom.

Here are only the orange trees
Drinking the wind ;
Drink first, and scent my cup.

Here is only my heart beating
And the opening of roses ;
Sing wicked and wanton,
Here are but nightingales.

Though you undress,
The moon and her lascivious little girls
Have seen before.

Though I kiss the points of your breasts,
The jasmin is accustomed,
The rose has seen before.

Lie naked,
Veiling your eyes in hair,
O jealousy of God.

40.

W E R E I to stay,
I'd see the places where her absence is
And hear her silences :
Let me away.

41.

I M A Y not sing
The beauties that lie hid by Izzat's dress
Beneath her coloured clothes,
Because my oaths
Have undertaken not to tell this thing.

If you could guess. . . .

If you could guess,
Ascetics in the dust of chastity,
You would bow down in bands
Between her hands
And worship her in mystical excess.

If you could see. . . .

Kusir.

42.

I, W H O grow the rose of sorrow
  By the pool of tears,
Do not know to what far country
  When the dawn appears
You will shape your vagabonding,
  Pilgrim of the years.

43.

F A R E W E L L Fatima, Neman's daughter,
  With a cadenced ostrich walk,
  And a waist of nabk stalk,
Teeth wet with the mouth's dew water.
Farewell fairness, a pool water,
  Farewell, Neman's daughter.

Farewell cheeks of surface silver,
  Golden wrists with copper bangles,
  Lake hair lying in black angles
Deep to drain my heart's bright river.
Farewell glorying glittering river,
  Farewell surface silver.

Dreams are the pictures in the book of sleep,
  And no more mine for ever.

Murakish.

44.

I CAME to a battle, a torment of red,
And asked of the dying :
' Ah, what is the prize ? '
Then one died sighing :
' A fair boy's eyes,'
And ' Eyes ' the smile of a dead man said.

45.

TELL him, O night,
How your black sword has killed my golden days
And your black brush obscured the smooth delight
About my eyes' dim ways.
    The breasts of my distress
Are pressed against the thorns of appetite,
Desire my food and my drink sleeplessness ;
    Tell him, O night.

46.

A LITTLE wicked city of Babylon
    Burns in each of her eyes,
The lights and swords and flowers of Babylon.

Over her neck of jasmin ivory
    Falls her hair's ebonies,
Night come visiting jasmin ivory.

Are they breasts of white flesh tenderly rounded
    Or hand-soft ivories
Or fruit like white flesh tenderly rounded?

White sand moving or moving thighs?

47.

W I N E's red in the cup,
A bird sings silver on the branches,
Life must be paid
So make life pay again.

This boy, my fair friend
Wine reddens and the white rose blanches,
Has heavy eyes.
I kissed a red rose once

On cheeks gay with Spring,
But, now light downs of youth enfranchise,
Peaches lie ripe
Where I thought a rose tree.

48.

A L L men shall rise on Resurrection Day
    Up to the sky,
Or when the pearl and almond you display,
    Sweet, of your thigh.

49.

T H O U G H the flames lick my heart over
And my soul is red with fever,
If you gave me choice of water
Or to see and burn for ever,
Sure, my burning ghost would wander
With a memory for lover,
With the Jewel, with the daughter
Of the sea king Salamander.

50.

I R A N G E D my grievances and came
    To where your golden eyes looked down ;
    I tried, but could not make a frown,
I tried, but could not hide a flame.

I wrote a commination
    Of things that proved that you were foul ;
    I stood there like a love-sick owl
And had forgotten every one.

51.

I F Y O U can call the sun and the moon and the rose-
        tree
Sad-coloured,
Call her sad-coloured also.

The river of life flows through the meadows of Eden,
And the meadows of Eden are below her garment,
The moon is beneath her mantle.

Her body is a song of colours :
Carnation of roses answers to silver,
Black ripe berries
And new-cut sandal-wood
Are one note.

The man who takes her is more blessed
Than the God who gives her ;
And He is continually called blessed.

52.

S A V E by his forehead and his hair
    We tell not day and night apart ;
Who then of his dark mole would dare
    To say it mars the roses' art ?
Or could the red anemone be fair
    Without her heart ?

53.

J O Y stays all night by your white side to sigh ;
    ' Now not an hour is wasted, Wahba.'
He knows the water of your mouth, which none but I
    Have tasted, Wahba.

He knows it rarer than the silver rain
   When thirst expects her visit, Wahba.
You brimmed its scarlet chalice once, and not again ;
   I miss it, Wahba.

Oh, be not like the fabled cock which lays
   Once in a lifetime only, Wahba ;
Come and perfume my dwelling, for the laggard days
   Are lonely, Wahba.

And bring that softer dew than morning's is
   Which weighs no tenderest fronds down, Wahba,
That dew more light than karkafa or kandaris
   Or swan's-down, Wahba.

54.

I SIPPED the rose-wine of his cheek
   And, having drunken hard
      Of so much sweet,
         Dressed only in a perfumed shift
   Of aromatic nard,
       Ran out, oh, mad, to lift
     Our love song in the street,
         Dressed only in a perfumed shift
   Of aromatic nard.

Abu Nowas

55.

T A K E this cup and drink this wine,
For it is a virgin wine
And the cup is new gold.

A woman who waits
Is the fool of time.

My nights have been many,
To see the brown waters of the Tigris
Under black-veiled stars
Or to watch the moon in the west
Thrusting her silver sword
Into the purple river.

56.

D R I N K at his mouth,
Forgetting the full red cups and reeling bowls.

Drink at his eyes,
Forgetting the purple scent of the vine.

Drink at his cheeks,
Forgetting the life of roses poured in crystal.

Drink at his heart,
Forgetting everything.

57.

Y O U have no hips
And you have cut your hair,
Also there lies a light shade even
Upon your lips.
Dear child, by these exceptions and this dearth
You'll have two kinds of lovers upon earth
And more in heaven.

Abu Nowas

58.

W H A T could my heart against the eyes
    Which throw gold cords on kings ?
The rose-fed wind of paradise
Stayed at your dark hair's garden spice
    To learn new perfumings ;
And the white stars came down with sighs
About your slim neck's argencies
    And danced into a ring.

59.

M O U R N over love's gold fire
Because my lover is pleasant to other women ;
But do not tell me to cease from adoring roses.

What shall a heart do
Which is stirred by roses ?

Here are twenty cups full of wine
And an old guitar for kisses,
But I have no myrrh.

My roses burn in the gold fire,
But there are others
And it is always spring in paradise.

Pray God, it is not a crime
To love so popular a creature.

60.

O N E look from your dark eyes
Viaticum supplies,
I take from my laſt kiss
Wine for all drynesses,
And from one smile
Food for a hundred mile.

61.

B Y arched bows that guard his eyes,
By their dark sweet treacheries,
By the white sword of his form
And his black hair's scented ſtorm,
By the laughing eyes which keep
Fires to burn the rose of sleep,
By curled scorpions of small hair
With bright ſtings to ſtab despair,
By the skin of apricot,
Silver feet which he has got ;
By the sun which rises pale,
By the moon, his finger-nail,
By ſtar and Spring, for he is both,
I charge myself to keep this oath.

62.

G O D breathed into a foam of pearl
And fashioned the beginnings of this girl,
After, He mingled myrtle with the dew
And took white roses, too ;
But in the end He had to add to these
All His bright gardens, all His wavering trees.

63.

Haroun's Favourite Song.

A N early dew woos the half-opened flowers,
    Wind of the south, dear child,
Close clings about their stalks for drunken hours ;
    And yet your eyes, dear child,
    Cool pools which rise, dear child,
        High in the mountains of my soul,
        These, these
    The lips have drunken whole ;
    And yet your mouth, dear child,
        Your mouth, dear child, is envied of the bees.

64.

M Y love was hardly circumcised
When spray of downy hairs surprised
(Eh, but I'm drunk) his cheeks.

The smiles upon his countenance
Are little fawns at lonely dance
(Eh, but I'm drunk) in Spring.

The wine that flows below his skin
Is a publican to call us in
(Eh, but I'm drunk) to sing.

Of all the charms below, above,
Those small green silken moulds I love,
(Eh, but I'm drunk) his breeks.

65.

W H A T do you in her garden, crow?
I can make all the harsh cries for this woe,
I would have you know.

66.

M Y dear
Is timid as a deer,
And yet a flying deer sometimes looks back.
My heart
Is given to a hart
Which snuffs the taint of love upon its track.
My hair
Is loosened for a hare,
A flying leaf, which lets me die of lack.

67.

O L O R D, who made her lips as honey sweet
Yet sharper than the sickle in the wheat,
  Grant me to be the honey to her steel,
O Lord, who made her to mow down the wheat ;
  O Lord, make me the carpet of her heel,
Who made the dream above her visiting feet.

O Lord, who cast the fullness of her hips
And made her spittle more than raisin drips,
  Favour the onyx tears I weep for her,
O Lord, who made her as the raisin drips.

O Lord, who made her roses on a stem
With golden starlight shining on to them,
  Grant that those roses pierce me to the heart,
O Lord, who made the starlight smile on them.

O Lord, who sent her as a silver mole
To fret my heart and tear into my soul,
  May she return to ravage them again,
O Lord, who made the body and the soul.

68.

*Hassan has seen the daughter of the King of the Jinn rise
up at dawn into the sky, after she has bathed.*

S H E came to tear my heart, and then above
   The sunrise the white mists have hidden her.
      (The morning dew received her, dressed in light.)
Who dare pretend that there is sweet in love ?
   If love be sweet, how more than sweet is myrrh.

69.

A W A T C H E R of the stars at night
Looked up and saw so rose and white
A boy, with such delicious grace,
Such brilliant tint of breast and face,
So curved and delicate of limb,
That he exclaimed on seeing him :
' Sure it was Saturn gave that hair,
A black star falling in the air ;
Those roses were a gift from Mars ;
The Archer of the seven stars
Gave all his arrows to that eye ;
While great sagacious Mercury
Did sweet intelligence impart,
Queen Venus forged his golden heart
And . . . and . . . '   But here the sage's art
Stopped short, and his old wits went wild
When the new star drew near and smiled.

70.

Y O U are more fair than a summer moon
  On a winter night, you are more fair.
  I said when I saw your falling hair :
' Night's black fain wing is hiding day.'
  ' A cloud, but lo ! the moon is there,'
You, rose child, found to say.

71.

*One day, as the warrior poet Dorayd rode near the
tents of the Solamides, he came upon Tumadir Al-Khansa,
daughter of Amr, a girl renowned in all the deserts for her
verses, anointing one of her father's camels with pitch.
As she laboured almost naked because of the heat, trusting
to the loneliness of that place, Dorayd improvised this song.*

S I N G to the Solamide,
  Sing for this Tumadir,
  Make for this light gazelle
Verses of pride !

Unveiled her young bloom,
  Never the riding tribes,
  Seeking a prodigy,
Found such a camel groom.

Brown girl of high race,
  Smooth as an image's
  Under the hair stream
Brightens her gold face.

STS-H

Like the black waves we see
   Tailing our stallions
   Is the wind-beaten tress.
Let to go carelessly

It floats in glancing chains ;
   When it is kissed with combs
   Then you would call it grapes
Polished by little rains.

Her brows are symmetries
   Drawn with a heavy pen,
   Black crowns of queenship
Over the deep eyes.

Modelled with leaf shadows,
   Her cheeks are scarce flecked,
   As by rose purple dawn
Rising on white meadows.

Her lips' red pigment
   Lends the small teeth pallor,
   Straight jasmin petals
Moistened in honey scent.

And the neck's silver, see,
   Balance above breasts
   Like the proud breasts on
Girls smoothed in ivory.

Her arms are firm for us,
    Firm for me, white for me,
    And of her finger-tips
Red dates are envious.

Belly with white valleys
    Folded of song paper,
    Ranged round the navel's
Deep box of essences !

Where can her waist borrow
    Strength for its slenderness
    When to such glory
Falls the slim back furrow ?

Mountains of white sands
    Drag her to sit on them,
    And when she would sit
Swift she again stands.

Yet on two slender
    Columns of smoothness,
    Stems of papyrus
Sprinkled with tender

Brown hair, two pearl stalks,
    Two filed and fine
    Feet that are lance blades,
The pride of her walks.

Sing to the Solamide,
   Sing for this Tumadir,
   Make for this light gazelle
Verses of pride !

72.

s h e rises with the burnished fruit
Of the Seven-pointed Archer,
A drop of gold among the steel of the stars,
A pearl announcing silver dawns,
Water flowing over silver,
A topaz with a gilded face,
The reincarnate ghost of all white roses.

73.

f o r very love I cannot speak ;
She sends for chess, her dreaming cheek
   Shines rose above the pieces.
I lose my head, I lose my queen,
I lose my heart : was never seen
   So quaint a game as this is.

I only take through skirmishing
A knight and rook, while my poor king
   At every point she teases ;
Yet I'd have triumphed after all
If we had but agreed to call
   Knights nights and castles kisses.

74.

I LOVED him when he had but roses ;
Only a fool supposes
I could forget
Now he has added myrtle, violet . . . .

75.

THE boy and girl have set
Their slender lips and kissed,
The gold procession of the sun has met
The silver journey of the moon,
The silver journey of the moon
Is lost within a crimson sunset mist.

76.

I DREAMED that Izzat and the sun stood still
    Before His chair whom beauty cannot blind,
He weighed their splendour with a patient skill
    And Izzat was the brighter to His mind.

Yet women dare to say she has a flaw. . . .
    May He who judged her perfect and complete
Break them in pieces utterly and straw
    Their cheeks as yellow roses for her feet.

Kusir.

77.

HER veil is torn from the bright blue
Which all the stars are hasting to,
Her lips control a hive of bees,
And roses are about her knees,
The white flakes of the jasmin twine
Round her twin sweetness carnaline,
Her waist is a slight reed which stands
Swayed on a hill of moving sands.

78.

BOAST, if you will, the magic chance
    Which took you safely through the fire ;
    A greater wonder I require
If you would parallel that glance
        Of jet,
        Which has not harmed me yet.

You tell me other cheeks can show
    Soft down as they approach a man's ;
    Not so the cheeks of my romance,
For that which I see over-grow
        Their milk
        Is ghost of gilded silk.

When we converse of magic streams
    Replete with youth-returning springs,
    You tell me there are no such things
And I am credulous it seems ;
        Yet I
        Would venture this reply :

The spring of youth's delightful joy
   Myself have tasted where it slips
   For ever from the dark red lips
Of a slim-waisted deer-swift boy,
     My tongue
     Remembers and is young.

79.

B R A V E child, who wins
Each skirmish in the battle of the roses,
   Your loot lies purple on your brow ;
And one supposes
   The captives of the garden now,
    The vanquished each and all,
    Lean down to kiss your feet, as small
And sweet as sins.

O princess maid,
The winds of evening get their sweet
By kissing your two feet.
   We have lost many a summer breeze
   Which ventured underneath your light chemise
And stayed.

80.

Y O U N G fawn with lighted eyes,
When you come near
It is as if my glances had drunken wine.

The light breeze of the desert
Is born scented when you sigh
At evening, at cool evening
Under the palm-trees.

I am offended with the west wind
Because he kisses you
And refreshes the scarlet langour of your cheeks.

Jasmin of his belly under vests,
White jasmin
Milky as moonstones !

The crimson flowers of his lips
Are watered with the water of his mouth,
His eyes close after love.

My heart flutters like a moth
About his body,
Heedless of arrows.

81.

BIN-SINAR in his book of cure
Says : ' Children, know that this is sure :
Love can be cured by constant song
And wine the garden side along.'
I took Bin-Sinar's sure advice
And came no nearer paradise ;

Therefore I set myself to try
A leaf from my own pharmacy,
And in a hundred sleepless nights
Assuaged as many appetites.
Sinar was wrong, for I can prove
Love is the only cure for love.

82.

G R E E N leaves as fairly shade the red pomegranate
    flowers,
    As you, your light chemise.
I ask its name which suits your golden cheek,
You ponder and then speak :
    ' It has no name, for it is my chemise.'
Yet I will call it murderer of ours,
    A murderous chemise. . . .

83.

T H E R E's a black Magus in her eyes
    And, if you miss his spell,
    There's a gold bowman there as well—
An arrow flies.

There's wine of fire within her voice,
    And you, who will not hear,
    May still be taken unaware
By two red toys.

84.

I H A V E those eyes of magic fire
That pierce through silk
To find desire :
        Balancing hips
        Like sailing ships,
Dimpled and dancing and white as milk ;
        Wavering breasts
        With crimson crests,
Like golden birds that shake their nests.

85.

G I V E him to me
And you shall have for fee
Blue burning diamonds from my treasury.

He was the moon
In night's blue burning noon,
Whose simplest words were songs to a low tune.

My prince of palms,
Whose branches in his calms
Bore golden-mannered speeches like gold psalms.

Enough of trees,
My child was more than these,
Himself blue burning noon and the relenting breeze.

86.

I A S K the rising sun for news,
I ask the evening star for tidings.

Sleep cannot tell me of you
And the wastes of the night cannot report of you.

My heart is a still green fen ;
Can you not come back
And make it run again in laughing water ?

Three Duets.

I.

I A M happy and light
Like a light dancer.

Breathe no more,
O lips red upon flutes ;
Be still,
Fingers on silver strings ;
That we may hear the palms.

The palms are girls
Standing under the night
And whispering to each other,
Their green hair dances
To the flute-playing of the west wind.

I am happy and light
Like a light dancer.

       Perfumed delight,
       The singing of your voice
       Builds up a palace of living marble
       For Him who bade love be beautiful,
       Perfumed delight.

You who are darkness about my eyes,
I will paint the lids of them azure
With a stick of crystal,
And in a bright paste of henna
Stain my fingers,
My hands shall be date-coloured
For your pleasure,
I shall burn a delicate incense
Below my breasts for
You who are darkness about my eyes.

2

GIRL,
It is raining flowers
And small coloured birds,
Let us wander with the wind
To warm Baghdad,
To the rose domes.

Not so, lord ;
Let us stay in the garden
Under the gold palms
And dream.

Girl,
Diamonds fall on the blue leaves,
The curves of the branches are beautiful
Against the sky.
Rise,
Shake the drops from your hair.

Not so, lord ;
Lay your head upon my knees,
Taste the flowers of my breast
Among my garments,
And listen to the light wind.

3.

I BRING light flowers
Under my veil of Kufa silk
And fruits still powdered with their gold.

All the gold of Sudan shines upon you,
O well-belov'd,
Because the sun has not ceased to kiss you.
The velvet of Damascus
Is woven from your past glances.

I come to you in the cool of the evening.
The light air
Stirs the blue veil of the night ;
There is a murmur of leaves and waters.

You are here,
Gazelle of nights :
My spirit dips towards your eyes
As a white bird to the sea.

Come near and take these roses ;
I slip like a flower
From the bud of my green silks.
I am naked for you.

Beloved !

I am here,
A young moon stealing to you through the trees,
A summer sea
Flown over by quick rejoicing birds.